About the author

Mara Sudol is an American poet, illustrator and author, living in Raleigh, North Carolina. Her work explores relationships, the human condition, romance, heartbreak, mental health and femininity. Mara credits her creative influences to the love, drugs and nightmares of New York City art school, LA lovers, the cocktail sippers at her bar, the gossip queens who adore her and her spunky dogs, Reo and Busy.

FOR GIRLS WHO CRY IN PUBLIC

MARA SUDOL

FOR GIRLS WHO CRY IN PUBLIC

Vanguard Press

VANGUARD PAPERBACK

© Copyright 2022
Mara Sudol

The right of Mara Sudol to be identified as author of
this work has been asserted by her in accordance with the
Copyright, Designs and Patents Act 1988.

All Rights Reserved

No reproduction, copy or transmission of this publication
may be made without written permission.
No paragraph of this publication may be reproduced,
copied or transmitted save with the written permission of the
publisher, or in accordance with the provisions
of the Copyright Act 1956 (as amended).

Any person who commits any unauthorised act in relation to
this publication may be liable to criminal
prosecution and civil claims for damages.

A CIP catalogue record for this title is
available from the British Library.

ISBN 978 1 80016 167 2

*Vanguard Press is an imprint of
Pegasus Elliot MacKenzie Publishers Ltd.*
www.pegasuspublishers.com

First Published in 2022

**Vanguard Press
Sheraton House Castle Park
Cambridge England**

Printed & Bound in Great Britain

Dedication

This book is dedicated to the many wonderful women in my life who have shown me the cathartic power of a good cry.

Acknowledgements

To my loving parents and brothers for supporting all of my wild endeavors; to my many muses over the years; to Emily, Lauren, Candice, Hannah, Gigi, Svet, Popov and all of my wonderful friends who have also supported my wild and wonderful ideas and for teaching me the power of being in touch with your feelings, both bad and good. To ex-boyfriends and ex-lovers, thank you for teaching me that there is way more out there in the world, and thank you for ghosting me so that I had something relatable to write about. Thank you to the wonderful women I've met over the years, you are far too many to name, for showing me that we are all in this together. Everybody feels, and collectively, we can feel together. And finally, a big thank you to my dogs, Reo and Busy, without whom life would not be possible. Thank you!

I remember having her around every day and the availability of her voice in the middle of the night. I remember the smell of salt and the weight of cold sheets on my bed. I remember the summer and slowly screaming words through the wind with my friends (and we were broken, still it's all that I want to do). I remember the old house and skipping school to lay in bed and take photographs of my life with sidewalk chalk. I remember crying on that bloody shoulder. I remember when the table had four chairs. I remember trying to fit eleven people on a stolen couch in an old stolen car. I remember when life was crowded and hot but simple and bright and everything echoed and no one minded and it was fun to take shortcuts through fountains in the middle of our city. I remember run on sentences and perfect punctuation. I remember unevenly spread cream cheese at midnight with my best friend. I remember when we loved just for the sake of loving. I remember sitting in the back of a cop car for the first time and laughing hysterically because there was a polaroid of human shit shoved in my underwear. I remember manic nights and dark dark days. I remember kisses on kitchen floors. I remember playing baseball with my dad on Tuesday nights. I remember the blurry boy who moved to Florida and ate cantaloupe in my tree house. I remember getting lost in a blizzard on Valentine's day, having nothing better to do than get out of the car and make snow angels. I remember getting grounded for coming home late. I remember having someone I loved nearby and the opportunity to call him and tell him 'I'm on my way over' in the middle of the night. I remember getting kissed because of the moon. I remember kissing back because of the stars. I remember strands of wet hair clinging to sun burnt cheeks. I remember sitting in my first love's garage and feeling beautiful for the first time in my entire life. I remember licking the walls because we thought they tasted like candy. I remember the bass thundering through our blood every single night. I remember my brother and I regularly running away and getting lost for hours with only the car stereo to save us. I remember coming home from detention and finding a note from my mom telling me she was leaving. I remember making everyone call me 'Lena' because that's what I wanted to be called. I remember singing *Under the Sea* with my best friend and jumping on our twin beds for hours. I remember a girl asking me to love her a little bit longer. I remember smiling casually and blinking once. I remember the feeling of dried Elmer's glue being peeled off of small elementary hands. I remember the smell of walnuts on my neighbor's workbench and running my fingers through boxes and boxes of useless bolts and nails to the sound of nineties grunge. I remember the day I stopped trusting. I remember the itchy feeling around my face after too many pills and piles of leaves. I remember swastikas in the backyard. I remember snowflakes on my lips. I remember the smell of my dad's cigars. I remember the tone of my mother's voice. I remember getting lost in Kmart and sitting down to cry in the picture frame aisle. I remember getting a crush on a boy because I drew a picture of the moon and he told me I could draw moons for the rest of my life, but he thought I would be happier drawing suns. I remember breathing on glass and learning to write backwards. I remember my mother spilling chicken noodle soup on her lap and the first time I ever saw her cry. I remember driving through the south in the backseat with my cousin and chasing UFOs to keep us awake, using the head rests as machine guns. I remember being carried through backyards by a boy because he thought I broke my ankle. I remember broken coffee cups. I remember not being mad at all that the air conditioner was broken in the car during that 104 degree car ride just because our skin was sticking to the leather seats and J Mascis was on the radio. I remember crawling through sewers for miles and miles. I remember laughing when my dad told me he was leaving. I remember Mulholland. I remember Ventura. I remember pink undershirts. I remember white tee-shirts. I remember birds. I remember warm water. I remember dry tears. I remember itchy noses. I remember small bags. I remember smiles. I remember funnel cake. I remember tumbling. I remember clarity.

I don't remember my birth mother's face or my first kiss.

for girls who cry in public

nostalgia;
love, and a reaction to some soft skin

melt here
twist there
mold into
me

it takes a while before
you can step over inert bodies
and go ahead with
what you were trying to do
in the beginning

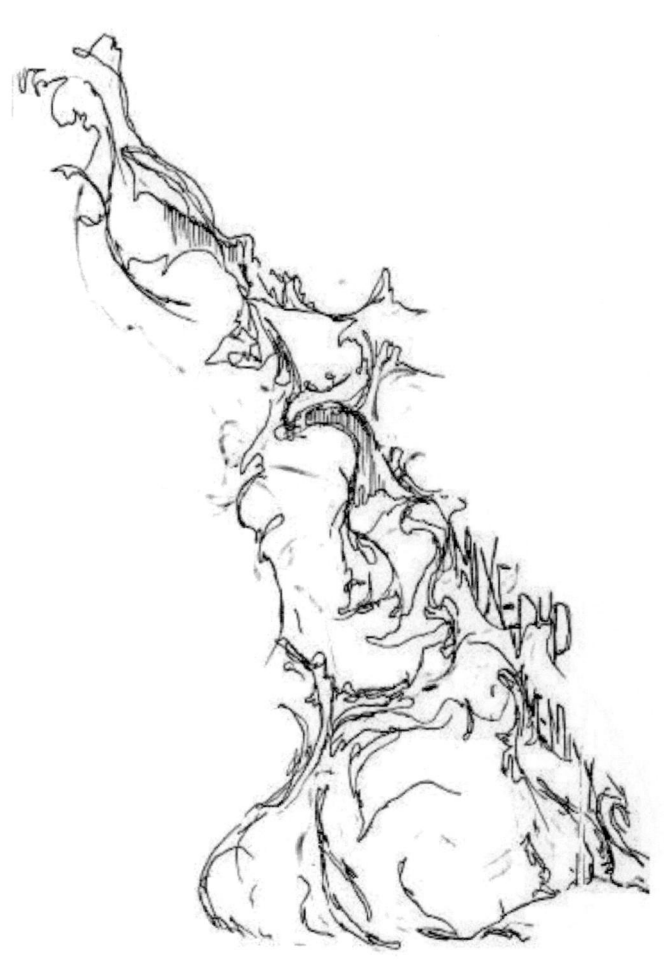

hollow hearts
cold hands
the way that you touch me
without hesitation
without conversation
you just know

that I smell my hair
when I'm nervous
and you like that
I'm nervous
around you
because just before
you become another ghost
we are the generation
that only loves
until three a.m.

if all I ever wanted
was what you wanted
would you want me

i went out looking for astronauts. i walk fast. you may say i walk too fast, but somebody once told me they'd marry me for my pace. so i walk even faster to avoid the cracks. just to be sure. always the bride, never the bridesmaid. i make wishes and watch them swim like fishes into the sky. i walk as slowly as i can. avoiding cracks. never looking back. it is my only plan. it is my only care. please don't stare. i know they are out there. astronauts. hovering. out of sync. above the horizon. below the low radar. graceful. shy. disconnected. watching the world from way up high. all my friends are astronauts.

i will not
fall in love
with your bones and skin
i will not fall in love
with the places you have been
i will not fall in love
with anything but the words
which flutter from your
extraordinary mind
there are moments in life
when a stunning angle
meets a timeworn curve
and beauty beckons another look.

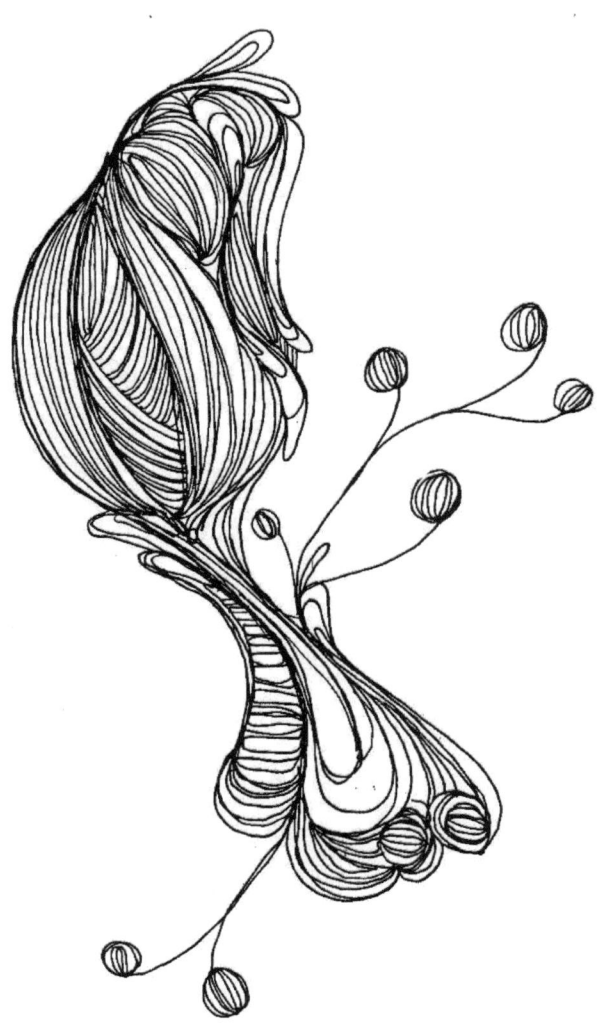

blood conscious
and aware of you
chaotically
the strange and treacherous softness
that always brings me back
to your arms

is it instinctive,
the way i seek you out?
the way my emotional rollercoaster
like the pull of the moon
always comes back

a mouth that was once intelligent
and softer than rolling thunderclouds,
your mind
so sensitively aware
takes over
your mind makes me drunk

the light in the garden
illuminated by moonlight
and the sound of you breathing;
the ghost in the hall
repeating patterns in circles
like your footsteps;
it's the exhaustion in the morning
after spending hours staring at your shadow
it's the scent in the air,
lingering with smoke
and the reflections in the kitchen;
walking into a crowded room,
meeting eyes with divinity and
seeing circles of spinning colors,
blood orange and crimson
seeing oblivion
the day we met

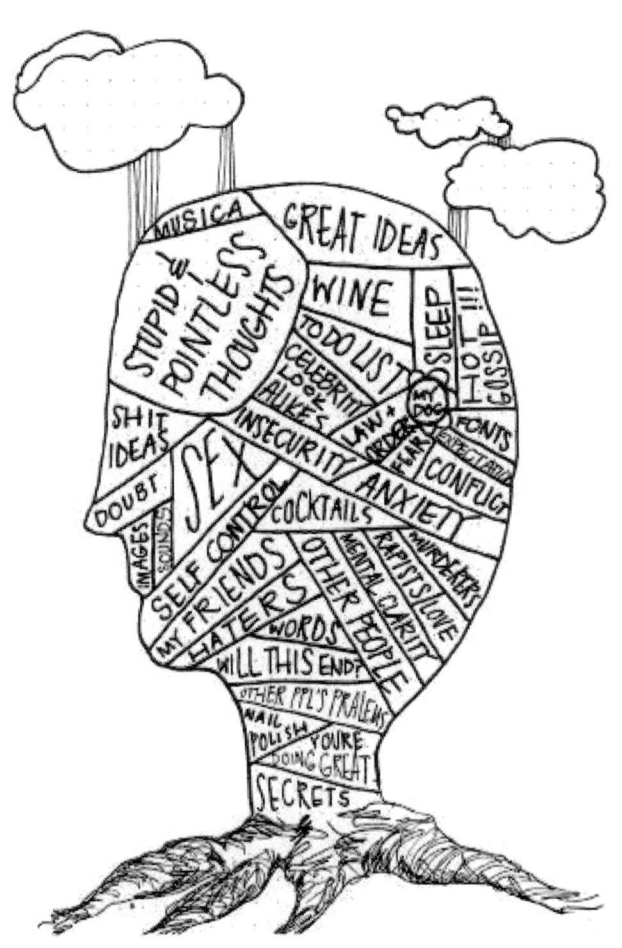

now better than fiction
your voice fills my head,
instead of theirs;
the song of the wild nights,
the mad to feel
the mad to love
the mad to live

you beat your head
against the walls of our world;
i will tear down veils,
i will consume
your vague and profound
wordlessness.

these hours called living;
a venomous mixture of
intellect and emotion,
rhetoric,
without the constraints of time.

you give me prickly heat.

surface mentalities
devil's details
truth's phenomena plastered
against grey
skies that illuminate only
the obsolete
as evidence
decayed
distant
diluted
quickly dilated
in a rush of logic
pull matter from verbose
quick reactions
slight of hand
the way this color flows
verbal fluidity
answer, answer, answer
react;
calm. quiet. detached. phased.
phase me.
the meaning has leaked
meaning only the meaningless
has skimmed the surface
of this fuzzy mental note,
mute.

some objects never travel
so they endure,
immune to oblivion
and the most strenuous labors
imposed by use and time
arrested in an eternity
of parallel instants that interweave
nothingness and habit
such a singular condition
poises them at the fringes
of life's tide and fever
this is where I sit
exhausted by the fight
to remain untroubled
by the doubt
the terror
faint and pointless
the duration

what i don't (cannot) know
sends shivers down my spine
like walking down the sidewalk on a sunday
morning
isolated
alone
wondering if you've missed a holiday
or you're just that numb
i want you to care
i want you to ask
i want to complain to my friends about
how you care way too much

i feel your colors
i feel your cinema
i feel what the motions will later look like spilled
out onto the pages
i feel you in film stills
and monologues
and i'll just never feel
you
i dream of you in colors that don't exist

running through the park at four a.m. with my best friends. life was crowded and hot and wet and messy but full of love and we didn't care. we are broken now but it's all that i want to do to hold on to the love.

hold my hand,
let's crawl through the ocean
lost in tangles
tied up
tangled up
in those thoughts,
those eyes
i'm reading you
the wasted days aren't yelling laments
through my walls
i swear i won't go back
just break those rules
and ignore the look on your face
the light in your eyes
when morning comes,
you are a mere definition
of a hand to hold
as we walk from the tide
completely free

the sounds that keep me awake;
raindrops outside of my window
from my bed, with a girl laying by my side
warm whispers,
the taste of salt from
stubborn tears and sweat
and strands of hair that stick to my face
in all of the wrong places
eyes that sing bewilderment and confusion
itch
not knowing the words
falling from quivering lips
sweet and soft skin
and the feeling of arms all around me
inspiration
running in the opposite direction
without shoes or a map
leaving ink stains in books
that aren't mine
losing control at the highest volume
secrets
dodging the nightmare
dodging the light
holding tears in my throat
wireless
milkshakes

the light of the morning
all of the words
that used to be pretty but have disappeared
tangled scarlet
spanish
singing into the wind
and goodbye kisses.
you are the sounds that keep me awake.

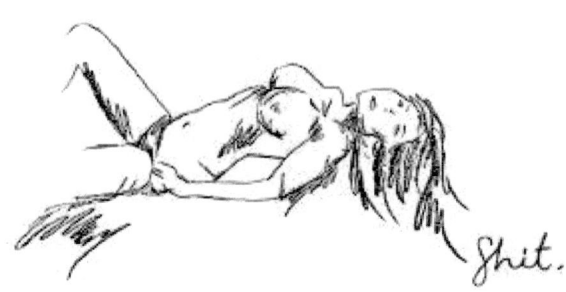

the swell, the rise
anticipation laced with doubt
wanting to say and do all of the right things
so badly that you end up
fucking.
up.
the swell.
coming together over a laugh
at whose expense?
glitter falling from your mouth
invincible
when there's no trust
and the glitter is what you
were attracted to in the first place
when sandpaper throats and ripped knees
meant honest and free
not loose and insecure
lost crushes
lost friends
lost secret lovers
losing yourself
and assurance
when what you felt
and how you used it
was right
because it was yours

but ownership
is a lie that we tell ourselves
right before the swell
at the bottom of the roller coaster
right when your body begins
to tip backwards
into inertia,
into the swell.

smoke plumes, thunderclouds
the sound of your voice
the pink haze that covers us at dawn
mixed with the smell of your hair
waves of warm nostalgia
like taking too many pills
and sitting in a hot bath
i'm trying to breathe
around you

looks like the sun
looks just like you
look like the sun

you're a five p.m. daydream
when my mind wanders off
wanders into thoughts of you
you're tequila
no salt, no lime
abrasive and acidic
yet you make me buzz
you're bad
you're good
you're warm

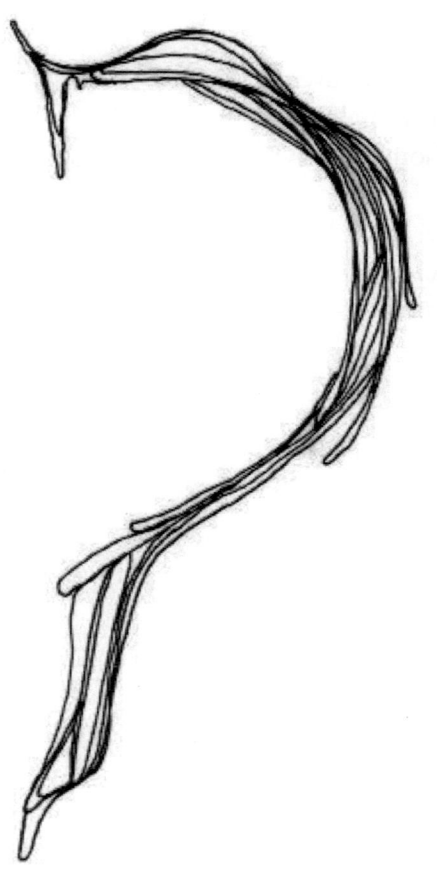

the unbearable feeling
of constant ideas
nice things
weird things
slow down please

love is the scars on your knees, the leftover pad thai in the refrigerator, the song that the birds sing in the morning, the pain you inflict, the sweet nothingness which flutters from your crush's mouth, a half smoked cigarette that you didn't want in the first place, diet coke with lemon fizzing on your tongue, the rainbow sprinkles on the cupcakes you never eat, the amazon package you received in the mail the other day, the sound of wind escaping through the new curtains, the dampness in your hair, the chipped red varnish on your fingernails, the music constantly playing in the background, the fingerprints on the walls, the bruises on your upper thigh, the bubblegum stuck to the bottom of your shoes, the tooth fairy and all of the things you wish you still believed in, your hands and all the things you can make with them, the kisses you blow, the clothes you wear, innocence, five a.m. morning breath, your sensitive teeth, the tingly feeling you get when you get touched on your neck, the tangles in your lover's hair, sleepless nights, sleeping pills, undeserved success, recognition, telling lies and not getting caught, blacking out, being desired by everyone at the same time, solving a problem, watching people around you, watching people fuck up around you, screaming off of the roof in the middle of the night, stalking your ex, make-up sex, smudged mascara, dewy sweat, disheveled hair, smeared lipstick, your morning coffee, silence, recyclable materials, trees, photosynthesis, growth, development. you, and i, and everyone we know. love is a careless mixture of all of the shit we constantly worry about.

i'm floating with the birds
i'm talking to the weeds
look at what you've done to me

the colors i see
right before falling asleep
life blurs into dreams of you
kissing my shoulder
in electric blue
and neon green
sweetness turns
to fiction

this is mostly impossible
mostly a secret
words you can't read
thoughts you can't touch
tangible illusion
save face, this time
tick tock
hearts race
stop the continuum
quit
cancel
exit
ending, engine
slow the fuck down
lightbulbs you can't see
phases you can't feel
melt and remold
a new book
a new reason
chest swells
let it in
let in this new life
lights aren't fading
bitter tastes like sour memories

sliding away with each passing
letter
pushed out
by each new word

saying 'I love you'

with that kaleidoscope vision,
you caught my attention
tenuous strands attached to the sky
caught like dreams on a kite
that I held in the palm of my hand
and with that icy tongue
and a language unknown to all others
you spoke sweet syllables
small thought, pure rhythms
tinted the shade of hot honey
that forced my eyes shut
now and again, I catch my chest
rising and falling
swelling with each
breath, word and sound, unspoken
like that space
caught in between
winter's curious chill
and summer's humid, moonlit kiss
a fleeting moment
a small glimpse of beauty
wrapped up
in the colorful filter of daybreak
I walk in and it steps back

dancing beside falling flames
disguised as warm rain
the repeated elegy
of some childish wish for lightning
and for morning to roll around again

if my sleep were an object,
it would be a worn and stained
sheet of stolen loose leaf paper
torn into itty bitty pieces
mixed up
flipped around
and sewn back together
with bits and pieces
of red thread
that is unravelling
before your eyes
you've been on my mind.

we've got to stay quiet,
follow me.
gothic blue, grey black, blood orange
startling lights
had their shadow dancers
carve beauty into brick
our ankles were wet
our breath was hot
our hands
locked
and eyes wide.
I saw solace and absolution
I heard both
truth and devastation
nuance and comfort
in harmony
with the shrinking earth
that had swallowed us whole
I was both small and immense
and both floating and alive
I saw the end, and it wrapped itself
under and around me
my skin was dizzy of touch
i saw motion,
with my eyes closed
wrapped around you.

sitting. waiting. watching. thinking. living. expanding. contradicting. listening interpreting. documenting. making. observing. strategizing. investigating. mixing. testing. experimenting. analysing. rendering. imagining. dreaming. traveling. wondering. reacting. acting. scheming. seeing. sensing. flowing. nesting. wanting. hoping. deconstructing. clearing. fixing. tracing. catastrophizing. trying. talking. admiring. litigating. looking. lamenting. elaborating. categorizing. compartmentalizing.

one molecule in the air
but potent enough
to define—
align your fingers,
and forget what you know.
stop believing in facts,
when relevance governs all;
you're erotic because you want to be
but desires are a necessity
when eating makes you cry
and kissing makes you cum
a mind without boundaries
we come undone.

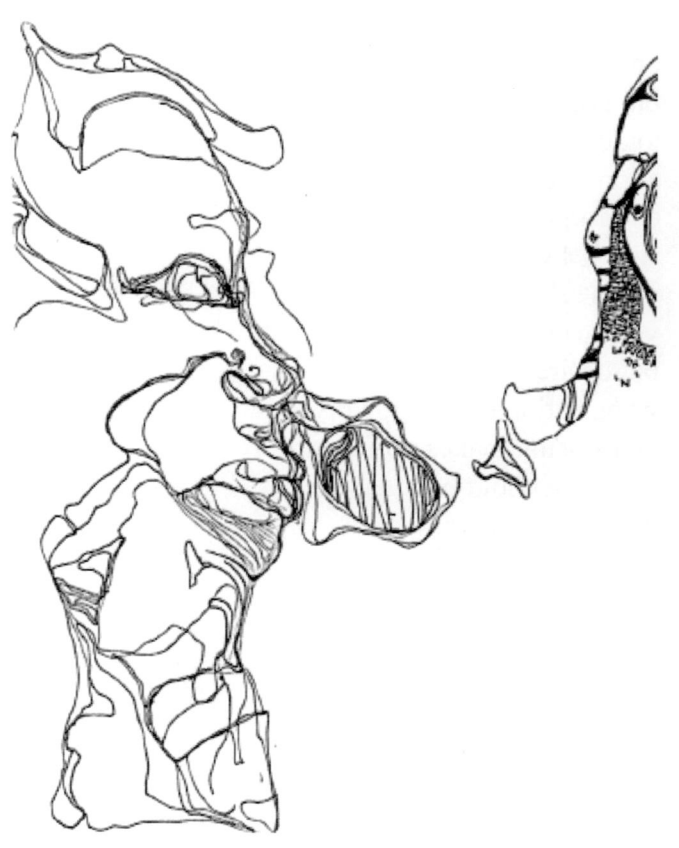

your beauty is archaic,
the way you monopolize
every part of my mind
and I smell you on my skin,
on my sheets, my clothes;
vague and undefined.
your voice
like a whisper through the wires
and here I stay,
a song caught in the distance,
some hope to admire.
you told me it's the sweets,
here in these sheets;
the sweepstakes prize
as you held my bones
shaky like a child's,
no room to move,
no room to run,
just the back and forth
of breathing patterns.
wild and worn,
mild and disregarding,
the universe unfolds.

I wish we could
just lie quietly
together,
and not have to worry
about all of the rest.

with no witnesses but the moon,
no task but to breathe.

verbose;
the united beats
of heat, sex and heartstrings
feeling out loud
and with words.

something to do with my hands
as the hurricane clears,
and the madness in our heads
rolls away.
with the dew in the morning grass,
it's five a.m.
when your kisses
are lazy, heavy, and deep
and neither you nor i
need to move mountains
and we stay intertwined,
with something to do
with our hands.

a silent presence;
intoxicated and inspired
sweet, slippery inspiration
as vivid as it is combustible.
outspoken siren,
raw fuel.
thicker than blood,
more potent than wine.
the venom,
the madness,
the hysteria,
the motion,
in the unknown
we are unstoppable

all day
filled with wet rain and thunder and
you've stayed up there
in my mind the whole time,
and I'd do anything
to hold you hot
against me
as my dewy skin
shows you all of the things
that I see.
palpitations.

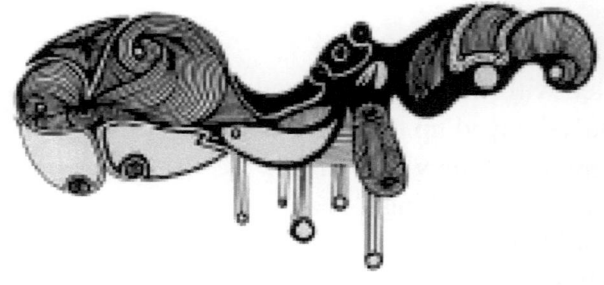

je prends de toi
ce que j'aime
pour prendre soin de toi

you.
you invade all aspects of my mind
constantly
you cover me and
I overthink
the sweet and simple things,
the complexities,
and dangle dangerously from you
like a loose thread.

there must be some road signs in this place. somewhere running in the dark in a crimson ballgown, spewing venom, vapor and truth, salty and disguised as water, it begins to overtake me in cascades like waves and starts to remake me into the pet that I was in the beginning.

rearrange her parts.

there is not
a single soul amongst the trees
and I,
don't know where I've gone;
look at what you've done to me.

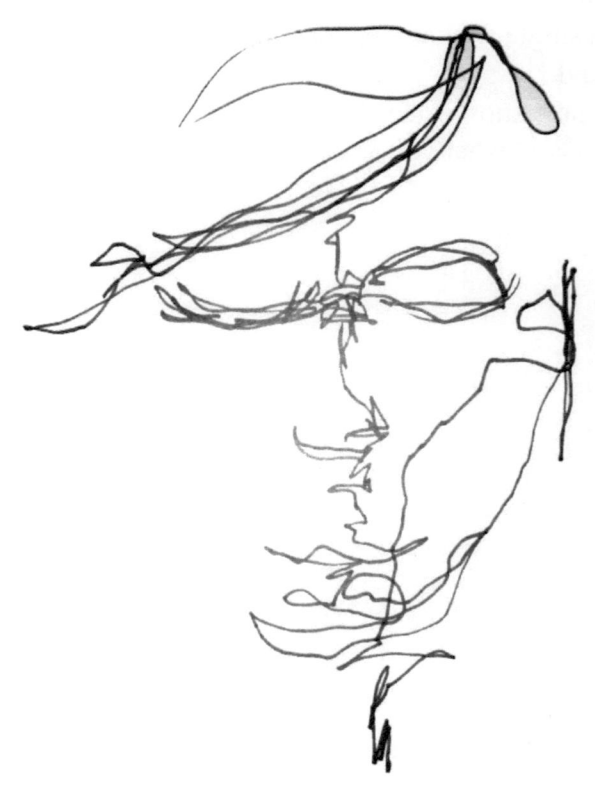

frequency showers
and cosmic riffs
the way you taste
mixed with the drip
of cold coffee
the morning after
i pull you out
from under sweaty sheets
heat lightening
cascading from your lips
tangled scarlet
and the scar you like to trace
with your perfect fingertips
good morning sounds like forever
in this storm

we rest
we rise
we feel
we open
we close
we die

i love you, i love you not.

i'd love to allow myself
to love you at the right volume;
at the volume
that kickstarts my heart,
that evens out
the mechanical hum
of the universe.
i'd love to tell you
what my tiny words cannot.
i'd love to show you what my
blind eyes and numbed touch
could never.
i'd love to tell you stories
of how I fell
three thousand feet underground;
underground and into you.
someday these thoughts
will crash,
and a furious lightning
storm of honesty
will erupt in their place

loves we had yet to learn existed
speaking in our secret tongues
in rhythm with the bass
thundering through our blood
eyes locked across the room
as i spin
in and out of consciousness
warm and wet and tingly
she's staring back at me
while you fuck me with your sullen gaze
all heavy eyelids and heavy arms
floating back and forth
in front of me
we come to
by the backdoor
backstage
surrounded by dirty leather chairs,
adrenaline junkies,
and the smell of shit cigarettes
and predetermined sex
you're floating
and i'm fading
in and out
i am, you are.

I am dancing with
my true love,
a memory of her;
she stands in the darkened wood
dizzying moonlight
warped and dripping
from the ebb and flow
the tides of her temperature
with eyes closed
I try to decipher it—
the screams that
get caught
in my throat

well now, fallen angel;
you, i'd say, are now lost.

and like water,
friction will run
hot blood
and wine on our lips
you bite your tongue
when we kiss
but those words,
i'll dismiss
i'll keep that
mouth busy

if I could close my eyes and see the ocean, see everything that its pulsing waves could swallow, I would put it into the four walls inside of my head. I'd see life, in all of its complexities; newness, growth, absence, solidarity, loss, pain, desire, serenity, and hunger. I'd hold on to them all and stand in the tide, with deep breaths of understanding and acceptance. I am at the edge of the world. I see it, and i'm okay.

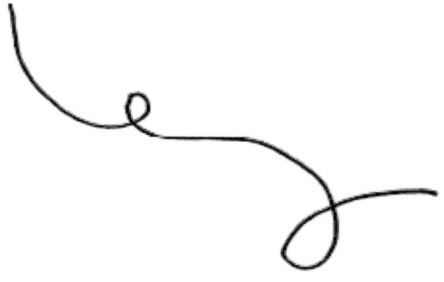

it, whatever that means or is
isn't a muse
isn't an idol
isn't a dream
isn't my own naivety
isn't a vision
isn't conceptual,
isn't literal
isn't a place to hide or feel
or fuck or run from
not a noun or a verb
but is every dissectible part
of each piece
and moment in time
amplified
and tossed towards the crimson sky
it's subliminal, it's subconscious,
it's painfully honest
and hard to read
it's right here,
just out of reach
racing towards
future volumes and frequencies
through the wide eyes
of some child
in the new morning snowfall

avoid nostalgia
and the onomatopoeia of
sound and sight
the purpose of your days
the passage of the world
the bane
of my existence

the universe
drowns in you

a tug of war between
gravity and the tide
my mouth and what is mine
like relativity or time
without boundaries
without limits
flying faster than the sound

and life is moving along
crawling past the cornerstone
and existence is starting to trickle
into somewhere I never
thought it would
and these syncopated heartbeats
are standing alone in rhythm
and I long to be, again
in sync with you,
whom I crawl to

the beginning of the end.

if only our tipped scales
were just
the changing of the seasons

here, where people converse and people mix and do the twist with the shades drawn tightly. one foot dancing and one foot out the door. a grand waltz where everybody cuts in, changes partners, and knows everybody on the dance floor's two step, can recite the steps to their waltz, and hum the tune to everybody else's tango. they move and shift shapes in the night, refusing to accept the truth of the matter; out of sight, out of words, out of mind.

i'm out the door
but if it makes you happy,
i'll keep clapping
all starry eyes
and glazed flames
dripping
she mentioned something about wednesday
but what do I know?
I killed them
your memories, your thoughts
your blood, your bones, your voice
your ghost
only slightly less than I'm used to
you get under my skin
I think I find it irritating
running to the sun
and we're taking it on
we're taking photos
or whatever you call it
I used to sometimes try to catch her
but now I mind my own business
and try not to look
at her
at the sun
but she's got a very lovely way with words

and i've got bones full of hate
but I try not to make a sound
so I sit and smile
and say
"oh, that's nice"
or whatever
down by the ocean
was full of ghosts and echoes,
but I wish I knew what I was looking for

you are not my idea,
you are my ideal.
i blanket myself
with a strength,
a vision available only with
you as my spiderweb.

lover,
lay me down
hover and
set me into motion.

scattered minds,
blended worlds.
that introspective, chaotic whirl.
nth degree,
constant state of flux;
i'm out of armor,
sweating dust.

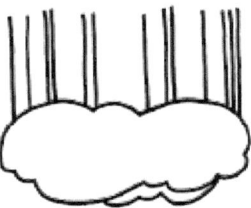

i'm here because i'm stuck here like a curious child caught in the quicksand. i'm here because i'm fragile, i'm weak. i'm here because my mind varies at the drop of a hat. i'm here because everything in life is guided by what you are capable of; to achieve, to accomplish, to make, to create. i'm here because i'm scared. i'm here because you left.

beauty rests
in one's own existence.
resistance,
resting on our tongues
like cool white wine.
written out like
her left handed scrawl,
until beams of light
again stand in our way
i am
you are.

fiction;
tell a lie that sounds like the truth.
tell a truth that nobody will believe.

i love you.

be my dialogue between
flesh and spirit
my midnight escape route,
my meandering lines,
my marble blues
and sunburnt reds.
be my place to fall;
beautiful fusion
of moving poetry
and time
blueprints,
and ultraviolet fingerprints
burned into
the back of my eyelids.

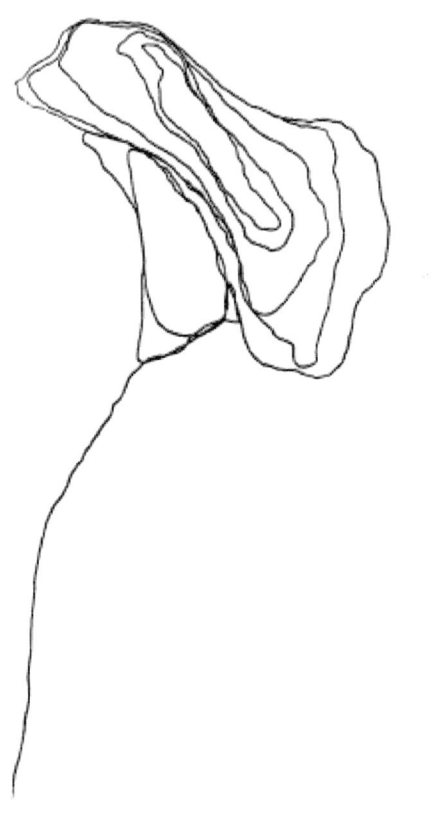

an obstacle
of light and motion;
and so it is
with only the white hot light
and screams of cold fiction

I hear my thoughts
loud and roaring
in soft hues
of mauve and purple

you play with my world
like it's your toy
you put a gun in my hand
and you hide from my eyes
but I see through your eyes
and I see through your brain
like I see through the water
that runs down my drain

I wonder if it burns
as words fly out so fast
once more
proving that we were more than that
acts of the hopeful
condescending in the end
when all I ever needed
was you to paint it black

and so now you're dating an actress, living in a studio in one of my memories, and you call every so often to make sure that i'm still alive, while you brag about how in love you are, and all of the celebrities that you serve coffee to. I try to sound like I believe you. I try to convince myself that I don't love you at all. I try not to let you hear the fact that I still cry when I think about birds, and the New York snowfalls. I try to believe that all of your tears were worth it.

the hours called living
the seductive mixture
of intellect and emotionalism
a rhetoric with no constraints
of time and fever
a laborious mosaic

because my mouth is a rushing river
because i'd probably say, "it happens"
because those birds never shut up
because the bottle never ends
because I did defend her
because sometimes I cannot differentiate the two
because I miss and I hate her
because my mind is mixed up
because of you.

beware of structure freaks. disrupters. adverbs. poets. monochrome. peacemakers. pizza ovens. hippies. mumblers. meeting skippers. people who fall asleep. lemonade. clowns. bobby kennedy. street fighters. scribbling. hustlers. people who admit that they're wrong. and those who know that they're right. pimps. nazis. puerto ricans. doing. changes. plans. postulates. ink stains. holy men. people who do everything. rules. expectations. soft lips. paper cuts. carnivals. limits. meditation. preparation. friends. horseshoe. cheap beer. euphemisms. pretence. high-deas. yoga teachers. fruity gum. fashionistas. telephone wires. anyone in a tunic. girls. gorillas. white noise. water guns. hand grenades. menthol. super glue. public restrooms. anywhere with a drive thru. the last piece of bread. gluten in general. diving boards. clocks. bunsen burners. agendas. wooden rulers. new year's eve. stimuli. coral reefs. too much knowledge. too much vodka. apathy. empathy. lust. lemon wedges. splinters. linoleum floors. chalkboards. jazz. pollination. hallucinations. digital reliance. the sunday comics. down comforters. red wine. visionaries. gypsies. facebook. twitter. sociopaths.

forever running
after the color
of golden, six o clock light
the color and time
when I start to feel alive
you said I wasn't crazy
that I was always goldenrod to you
and she just sings about
some distant blue ocean
that we used to call home,
strumming the same sad chords
we trade liquor for blood
in an attempt to tip
the scales.

chance;
the things that
shift our vision
our perspective
shift focus,
shift shapes
the tiny things
that perhaps are meaningless
to all else
are all that sustain me
i'm in a space
where my mind
is at the center of the madness
the maelstrom
squint at the world;
see more
while you are seeing less

maybe I keep falling for it—
either way,
the universe is a hypocrite

sad boy's club.
i remember the back of your mind
i remember the sounds that don't mean shit to me now
i remember houses with nobody in them
i remember ignition
i remember dry hands
i remember that park and what you wanted to do in it
i remember my shoes on the dash
i remember you scolding me for them being there
i remember vodka sodas in the afternoon
i remember the first time you were in my house
i remember wet paint and bedroom music
i remember catching all of the lights
and hearing,
"keep smiling, sunshine,
you're okay"

retracing my steps
all the way back
to commune with the dead
they said
you'd look better alive
i think you lost
what you loved most
in that mess of details.

because it is a two letter word
because understanding takes practice
because I need a place to fall
because I was bashful with the trees
because it was a shitty winter
because red is intoxicating
because of the raging war
because everybody looked so fucking friendly that I ran away
because it was a grey room
because the dream czar shook hands with orion
because I can't always know
because a door in the sky opened
because going nowhere takes a long time when there is nothing to say
because my hands hear the earth talking and the world sign
because I didn't say so
because it just is
because circumstance takes my breath away

dear girl,
we are alone in this world.

to fully live a life
on impulse,
on emotion,
riding the coattails
of that white hot heat
is exhausting
yet, it's the only way
that I can understand
to come up for air
and make sense of the world
right before I go
under again

to alter your imagination
that is the wildest power
to have over a person
romance outlasts the realistic
we forget about
our beautiful possessions
beautiful things
and bodies and souls
once yearning takes hold
and all you can do
is fantasize
romanticize
about the first woman you wanted
even if she was the last
allure is a tricky fuck
when you least expect it
your imagination has been altered
and you will never again be healed
you will never love again.

laugh into the darkness
like she laughs at her days
skimming fictions for hours
her voice clear
like the lonely window that looks up
to the moon
to the sky
to the answers to her questions
once full of desire
now gone too soon
left wrinkled
left cracked
too hot and too far
we beg for the strength to spell
out for us the answers
witless comments and monotone concerns
what urgency lacks
in this distant state
distance?
states and this state
her state of heart
my state of mind
the love she craves
fluidly drips into her days
boredom
when she creeps in

i slowly crawl out,
glowing
the ghost of a third person
crawling into my side of the bed
her apathy is deafening
tell me what I long to hear
tell me an explanation
and yes, this all makes me fucking sick.

I don't love you less
to love you more
I need you and me and her and him
at all parts
of the day
two beings,
all intertwined
because I bring you experience
and stories
it's how I sustain
and I am grateful
that you feed it
I stay loyal to my muses.

I ripped out the pages
of the thoughts i'm not supposed to think
emotional leftovers
and truth smeared ink
such an easy transition
from in love
to in lust
for you, not I
i'm sorry
for all of these stubborn tears
you are emotionless
and here I am, cascading
maybe i've built up mountains
maybe my walls are too weak
but the water keeps flowing
there's bound to be a leak
i'm trying to be your friend
your absent, superficial friend
take me for
what i cannot ever be.

gradually, and then all of a sudden
i really hurt myself
the cat scratches
and they come back
like a dot that becomes a thought bubble
and goes for a walk
after midnight
gradually, and then suddenly
it comes back
as expected
the blood; blackout and warped
the cold chills
nouns and verbs
and backwards, cursive screams
that come racing out of your throat
at three a.m. when you're done fucking
your new friend
and nobody feels a thing
coffee rants
out of their mouths
into yours
your voice and your mind
emotional torture
like that acid trip last winter
and you sit
cold and annoyed

and wonder
why this is constantly on repeat
i did it again
it's only me

feeling something
better than this
bitter taste in the back of my throat
better than the hatred ridden on my fingertips
feeling something
alive
and dead at the same time
comatose and ready to live
feeling numb
is better than feeling this
empty
he thinks i'm lying
i think i'm hiding from the truth
there is no difference, I suppose
one hurts you the same as the other
i'd rather feel numb
than feel the reverb
of this life

some days are endless blizzards, and some nights never stop. some worlds collide into colorful sunrises, freckled with the here, the there, and the somewhat. sometimes i want to know, i want to know, i fucking want to know. sometimes i beg for ignorance. sometimes i beg for changing lanes and hours. some friends never change a stitch or leave your side, but instead grow feverishly stronger with the passing of time. some things don't stop, some noises don't dull. sometimes tears are able to stay indifferent to the cause, reaction and reason, just like the wind. some shifts fit together, and some are pre-shrunk.

everybody in the room was feeling it, alive and nerves glowing.
i thought the walls were on fire.

secrets, masquerades, silence, and honest to god spontaneity.

rhythm is a stubborn fuck.

if I could, I would
excavation, hibernation
i'd break inside
against all will
just to figure this mess
i've found myself in
if i could, for you, i would
but I wouldn't know where
to begin sorting through
the DNA trapped inside of me
planted, locked, growing
that once did, and still does
belong to you

goodbye

aquamarine,
amethyst,
violet indigo,
turquoise.
it's astonishing;
the optical equivalent
of the cymbals being clashed
beside your ear.
it is so blue
when you look at it,
your skull feels hollow.
such love
is a monster.

how many times
must we feel this on repeat
contemplating the night's bright stars
and our battle wounds
a shaharazade of wakeup calls
and immediate excuses
no, i'll never see you again
no, i never loved you
no, i never tried

come and dust these shelves
and reveal the truth
of secret affairs
and wallow in someone else's apathy

ours are gifts for life itself
for an unfortunately astute
understanding of all of the pain
all of the messiness
within the world.
let's stay
full of crazy ideas
and grandiloquent needs
and a bit of happiness.

turn the page, a new day
with eyes wide and weary
I write what I am told
by the motion of your eyelashes
and with conviction
I enter you
the truthfulness of the dark
but I want proofs of the darkness
I want to drink that black wine
take my eyes and crush them
a drop of this vacuous night
dances and lands
on my naked quivering skin
mysteries of carnation
closing your heavy eyelids
i open them inside
always awake
on a bed of scarlet
your wet tongue
warm mouth
and the effigies that fall from it
there are fountains
in the garden of your veins
with a mask of blood
I cross your thoughts blankly
and amnesia guides me over to your side

I dream
as you paint my body
it's like licking a rainbow
all nerves and skin
wake up
it's time to run

borders
crossing borderlines
like fences in my head
I don't think it's time
to cross them
so take me down
in between lost
and i've been found
in this strange town
with no people
only drugged up ghosts
I just sleepwalk half alive
nine feet up,
six states away
love come and gone
yet I still stay
next to the wishbone
in my locket
stolen shoelaces
stuffed in my pocket

bathroom kisses
the smell of your cologne
lingering in the hall
after i kiss you goodbye
and we promise each other
little white lies

i believe in fiction & A symmetry

i am dancing with
my true love,
a memory of her;
she stands in the darkened wood
dizzying moonlight
warped and dripping
from the ebb and flow
the tides of her temperature
with eyes closed
i try to decipher it —
the screams that
get caught
in my throat

you're the goodness that came
and the rush of the flame
you're the gauge full of pressure
that's filled with my heart
you're the quick shift
from dark into light
you're the start of a smile
you're the cause of a scream
every emotion running through
my twisted and fucked up head
you're everything i swallow
every curse I scream
every flower
I insist on picking even though
you tell me she will only die
every song I sing
and now un-sing
you used to be every breeze
now you fill my nightmares
with every empty chill
you're everything that we tried
to convince each other we were not.

without you here
in my arms
all that is left to do
is to sustain

all that remains
is the leftover ecstasy
in the places that stay
empty without your warmth
defenseless
scratch across the moon, darling
carve it into my mind

i want you
i need you
i hate you
text me back
i can't stand you
talk to me
stop texting me
fuck me
love me
hate me
i love you

modern romance

in the end
we all lose interest anyhow
so I didn't feel the need
to finish.

and she
a mere relic of that cold war
a battle my bones are bending for
I won't waste time
trying to relocate my body
from this vague abundance
of crimson sand
red sailor,
tip the tides on me

i'm not sorry for
what's not written across my face
i'm not sorry for
the whirlwind
that has taken its place

tonight it's too quiet
so I push all of your old numbers
until I wake your ghost

we're getting back
back to the seven a.m. golden light
late nights of nonsense ideas
the feeling of bones
the taste of hunger
the sound
of all of the dimensions
coming together
in one hot instant
the sound of awe
coming from
every corner of the room
i'm getting back
to me

www.ingramcontent.com/pod-product-compliance
Ingram Content Group UK Ltd.
Pitfield, Milton Keynes, MK11 3LW, UK
UKHW041943230426
12048UKWH00008B/100